Oceans Apart

Written & Illustrated by
Hallie Darnall and
Haley Villont

Oceans Apart
Copyright © Never Forget
Publishing 2013

Special thanks to the student designers at Augustana College and particularly to Jasen Hengst for his focus on developing a brand image that is consistent with our mission.

A BOOK by ME
Holocaust Series

History comes alive with true stories written by children for children

A BOOK by ME is dedicated to the Quad Cities' Three Esthers

Esther Avruch   **Esther Katz**   **Esther Schiff**

Also, lovingly dedicated to Ida Kramer, Holocaust Historian, & Edith Levy, Jewish Holocaust Survivor & Author

MISSION STATEMENT:
A BOOK by ME® seeks to preserve the history of the Holocaust and other human rights issues. Our desire is to preserve the stories for the next generation so lessons of tolerance, empathy, hope and respect are not lost.

Deb Bowen's work with young authors is important for our generation and the next. Without her, some stories may have gotten lost. Her work is geared towards realization and understanding, hence, prevention. I fully believe in the importance of her work for generations to come.

Dr. Edith Rechter Levy, Ph.D
Holocaust Survivor, Author and Scholar

Dear Reader,

This is a true story about a famous Jewish girl named Anne Frank and her pen pal from Iowa named Juanita Wagner (pictured below). Juanita's teacher, Birdie Mathews, was a world traveler who experienced life abroad. She wanted her students to learn about new cultures by having pen pals. Young Juanita drew the name of ten-year-old Anne Frank. This fostered a friendship that ended abruptly once the Nazis occupied Amsterdam forcing the Franks into hiding. Here are some facts we learned about Juanita as we began to research her:

Name: Juanita Wagner

Born: Danville, Iowa

Family: Mother and sister Betty Ann
          (Father passed away)

Story: A creative, rural school teacher brought Anne Frank into Juanita's life. Before the Frank family went into hiding, the girl's letters went back and forth across the Atlantic Ocean. In addition, Betty Ann, Juanita's sister, began writing back and forth with Anne's older sister Margot.

We hope this book brings Anne Frank to life for students across the United States. It's incredible just knowing she had an American connection; to the cornfields of Iowa, of all places. It's especially exciting to us that Anne knew where our hometown of Burlington was when she found it on a map.

This book is dedicated to teachers everywhere but especially "Miss Birdie," Juanita's amazing teacher in Danville. Also, it is dedicated to Katie Salisbury, our teacher, who discovered and shared this writing opportunity called A BOOK by ME® with us.

Yours Truly,
Hallie Darnall and Haley Villont
Burlington, Iowa

As I sat in Miss Birdie's classroom, my mind began to wander. "Juanita, are you listening?" Miss Birdie asked. "We're going to be writing to pen pals. Each of you will have an opportunity to communicate with someone from a different place, even overseas if you'd like."

After Miss Birdie finished explaining, we each took turns drawing names. As I pulled out the slip of paper, it was as if there were millions of butterflies in my stomach. I slowly read the name written on my paper: Anne Frank. I sat down at my desk, somewhat relieved my pen pal was a girl. I pulled out my piece of paper and began writing. I didn't know exactly what to say, so I filled my page with things about me, my family, and small talk.

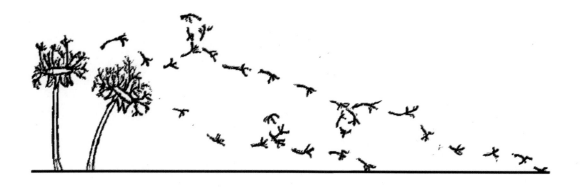

I anxiously waited for Anne to write back. I couldn't wait to learn about her, and find out if she liked the same things as I did. I waited and waited. Finally, one day, I got my reply. As I slid my fingers over the thin paper envelope, the same butterflies I felt before fluttered in my stomach.

In Anne's letter, she told me about her family and what she liked to do in her spare time. One thing that puzzled me was that the letter was written in English. I didn't think too much of it, and I quickly replied.

Years flew by with no word from Anne. I waited for a very long time, hoping for a letter to arrive. No letter ever came.

I grew up, as any little girl does, married, and eventually gave the letters to my sister, Betty Ann. I still wondered what had happened to my Dutch friend. As time passed, I thought less and less about Anne and the letters, until one day, I got an exciting phone call from Betty Ann.

She explained that she'd written a letter to the address we'd had for Anne, and she'd heard back from Anne's father, Otto Frank. Curiosity overcame me, as I waited patiently for the answer I thought I would never get.

Anne's father's letter had explained that during the war they had been taken to a concentration camp because they were Jewish. He told of their trials and what they'd been through. The letter gave us the answer that both my sister and I had always wondered about: What happened to the Franks?

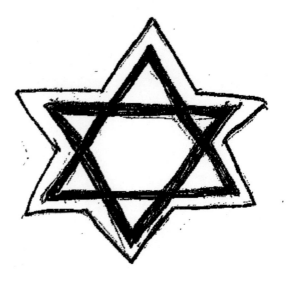

Anne and her sister Margot had both died in the concentration camp. Anne had kept a journal of her experiences while the Franks were in hiding. They had hid from the Nazis for a very long time in an attic of a building before they had been taken to the camp. This was the reason Anne had never replied to my letter.

My experience writing with Anne was short lived, but it was something that I will never forget. I still look back on that one experience in my life with amazement. A small town girl from Danville, Iowa, being pen pals with Anne Frank, someone who would come to be one of the most well-known faces of the Holocaust. What are the odds?

From the Family Album

Anne Frank

Juanita Wagner

Margot Frank

Betty Ann Wagner

"Everyone has inside of him a piece of good news. The good news is that you don't know how great you can be! How much you can love! What you can accomplish! And what your potential is!"

"Where there's hope, there's life. It fills us with fresh courage and makes us strong again."

Come visit our Anne Frank exhibit at 102 North Main Street in Danville, Iowa.

"Despite everything, I believe that people are really good at heart."

11

Juanita Wagner
Anne Frank's Iowa Pen Pal

One spring day in 1940, the seventh and eighth grade teacher Birdie Mathews, at the Danville Community School in Des Moines County offered her students the chance to correspond with pen pals overseas. A student named Juanita Wagner drew the name of a ten-year-old girl in the Netherlands— Anne Frank.

The name Anne Frank is familiar to us today because of the famous diary the young Jewish girl kept while in hiding from the Nazis. Her diary describes the usual adolescent fears about growing up, falling in love and being misunderstood by her parents. Yet, she also writes as a Jew hiding from the Nazis. Readers of the diary all over the world have come to see her as a heroine of the war because, in spite of all she suffered, she still felt that people were inherently "good at heart."

The brief connection between Amsterdam and Danville was the work of Birdie Mathews. By 1940, Mathews was a veteran teacher. She had been teaching since age eighteen, beginning her career at nearby Plank Road rural school. Around 1921, she moved to the Danville Community School after over two decades at a country school. She had already taught a wide range of curriculum and varying ages and levels of students. No doubt this had made her a seasoned teacher who had overcome the professional isolation that often plagued rural and small town teachers.

In this period of time, teachers had few opportunities to interact with colleagues outside of their buildings. Even help from the Iowa State Department of Education seemed distant and limited. In an effort to bring new teaching practices and ideas to rural teachers, the University of Iowa and other colleges brought traveling workshops called Tri-County Institutes to regional locations. The institutes met for a half or whole day session of speakers and workshops. The institutes minimized the isolation of rural teachers and furthered their professional growth.

"Miss Birdie," as her students called her, acquired more teaching resources through travel. She was even a bit of a local celebrity when she sent home lengthy letters to the *Danville Enterprise* sharing stories of her 1914 trip to Europe. Her letters became front-page news, and her travel experiences became classroom lesson plans. Her students often spent afternoons gathering around Mathews to hear about her adventures. In order to open their eyes to the world beyond, she frequently sent postcards to her students from her travels overseas and across the country. It is believed that on one of these trips she acquired the names of potential pen pals for her students.

Because pen-pal writing as classroom practice was still fairly rare at this time, only creative teachers such as Birdie Mathews would have set up situations in which their students could learn first-hand about the world. Some Danville students wrote to other children in the United States, but many, including Juanita Wagner, chose to write to overseas pen pals. In her introductory letter in the spring of 1940,

Juanita, age ten, wrote about Iowa, her mother (a teacher), sister Betty Ann, life on their farm and in nearby Danville. She sealed the letter and sent it to Anne Frank's address in Amsterdam.

In a few weeks, Juanita received not one, but two overseas letters. Anne had written back to Juanita, and Anne's sister Margot, age fourteen had written a letter to Betty Ann, Juanita's fourteen-year-old sister. "It was such a special joy as a child to have the experience of receiving a letter from a pen pal overseas," Betty Ann Wagner later recalled. "In those days we had no TV, little radio, and maybe a newspaper once or twice a week. Living on a farm with so little communication could be very dull except for all the good books from the library."

The Frank sisters' letters from Amsterdam were dated April 27, 1940 and April 29, 1940 and were written in ink on light blue stationary. Anne and Margot had enclosed their school pictures. The letters were in English, but experts believe that the Frank sisters probably first composed their letters in Dutch and then copied them over in English after their father, Otto Frank, translated them.

In her letter, Anne told of her family, her Montessori school, and Amsterdam. She must have pulled out a map of the United States because she wrote, "On the map I looked again and found the name Burlington." Enclosing a postcard of Amsterdam, she mentioned her hobby of picture-card collecting. "I have already about 800."

After the war was over, Betty Ann Wagner was teaching in a country school in eastern Illinois. Still curious about the Dutch pen pals, she wrote again to Anne's address in Amsterdam. A few months later, she received a long, handwritten letter from Otto Frank. He told about the family hiding, of Anne's experiences in the "secret annex" and how Anne had died in a concentration camp. This was the first time Betty Ann learned that Anne had been Jewish. "When I received the letter, I shed tears," Betty Ann recalled. "The next day I took it with me to school and read Otto Frank's letter to my students. I wanted them to realize how fortunate they were to be in America during World War II." - See Anne Frank's letter to Juanita Wagner at www.traces.org/anne

Students at Danville schools launched a postcard campaign in December of 2012. They are asking people to send postcards in honor of Anne and the 1.5 million Jewish children who died in the Holocaust.

Send postcards to:
Danville Schools • 419 S Main Street • Danville, Iowa • 52623

Their goal is to collect 1.5 million postcards.

*"Once I really am in power, my first and foremost task will be the annihilation of the Jews." * -Adolf Hitler*
Hitler's words in 1922, according to Major Josef Hell, a German journalist in the 20s and 30s

About the Author/Illustrator
Haley Villont

Haley Villont is now a sophomore in high school. She loves to write, and it has been her dream to become a published author by the age of 19. Her grandfather was a World War II veteran and always encouraged her to follow her dreams and shoot for the moon. She knows he would be proud of her and would like to dedicate this work to him.

While visiting from Arizona, Paige and Brook Betz (Haley's cousins) were used as models to represent the Wagner sisters.

About the Author/Illustrator
Hallie Darnall

Hallie Darnall recently moved back into the district from Florida and recalls the joys of writing to old friends far away. Writing this book helped her recall those memories.

The authors are high school students from the Burlington Community School District. They both enjoy writing and photography in their spare time. Both girls have helped their extended learning teacher write a monthly student newspaper and school newsletter. The girls are thankful for this opportunity to work together to create this book and share this story with others.

To find out more about the Anne Frank Iowa project go to (Anne Frank's Iowa pen pal) at www.abookbyme.com.

LEARNING STATION

Vocabulary and Key Terms

anxiously – uneasiness of mind, worried

attic – a room or space directly below the roof of a building

concentration camp – a guarded place where prisoners are confined and forced to work

curiosity – desire to know, interest in others' concerns

Dutch – a person from Holland or the Netherlands, or a Germanic country

Holocaust – the killing of six million European Jews and millions of other selected groups during World War II (also known as The Shoah)

Jew - an ethnic and religious group of people

overseas – beyond or across the ocean

puzzled – to be uncertain as to action or a problem

relieved – removal of something oppressive, painful or distressing

wander – to move or walk without an aim

Short Summary

A young girl, living in Amsterdam, by the name of Anne Frank was asked if she would like to have an American pen pal. She said yes. This is how Anne's name and address was drawn by a girl named Juanita Wagner from Danville, Iowa. Not only did these two girls begin a friendship but also their older sisters Margot and Betty Ann began to write each other as well. Find out about Anne from the perspective of an Iowa girl.

MLA Citation

Darnall, Hallie and Villont, Haley. *Oceans Apart*. Vol. 38. Aledo, IL: Never Forget, 2013. Print. Holocaust Ser.

Topics Covered

Acceptance
Anti-Bullying
Anti-Semitism
Holocaust
Hope
Perseverance
WWII History

LEARNING STATION

Thinking Strategies

- Making Connections – Connect the reading to the existing schema.
- Questioning – Question before, during, and after reading. Consider the content, ideas, and events.
- Visualizing – Use background knowledge, make mental pictures of the text.
- Inferring – Use knowledge to infer the underlying theme or idea to interpret meaning.
- Determining Importance – Develop summarizing skills.
- Synthesizing – Make sense of important information to construct deeper meaning.

Pre-Reading Discussion

- What is a pen pal? A pen pal is defined as a friend made and kept through correspondence.
- Why is having a pen pal useful or educational? Have you ever had a pen pal? If so, did you enjoy the experience?
- How do you think the idea of "pen pals" and the Holocaust could be connected in the book Oceans Apart? Make a prediction.

Pre-Reading Activities

Make a KWL chart on what the students know about the most well-known face of the Holocaust: Anne Frank. In the first section, write what they already know. In the second, what they want to learn. Save the last section for what they learned after the unit.

Know	Want to know	Learned

Related Literature & Media

A BOOK by ME Holocaust Series *
- Book #7 *Hide and Seek with Evil* tells the story of two German-Jewish girls who tried to hide from Hitler.
- Book #22 *The Tailor's Life* is a story about a young boy who survives Auschwitz concentration camp.
- Book #37 *A Secret Journey: The Courageous Story of Art Hilmo* tells the incredible story of a teenage boy from Norway who risks his life to ski refugees to safety in Sweden.

Other Books *
- *The Diary of Anne Frank* by Anne Frank is the published diary of a young girl in Amsterdam. It is recommended for grades 6-8.
- *Anne Frank: Beyond the Diary – A Photographic Remembrance* by Ruud Van der Rol and Rian Verhoeven is recommended for grades 5 and up. It includes quotes from the diary, photographs that have never been published and expanded descriptions about the economic times all while following the life of Anne Frank.

*Preview all literature for appropriateness for the age group

Technology

Have students write mini-book reports to post on the A BOOK by ME Facebook page where others will read about their opinion of the story. Review with students how to write descriptions and to summarize. Include the theme and lessons learned. Remind students to be respectful in their writings. All posts on the Facebook page will be monitored.

 facebook.com / A BOOK by ME

LEARNING STATION

Discussion Questions

1) When Ms. Birdie told the class that they would be writing to pen pals, Juanita gets nervous. Why do you think she was nervous? How would you feel if you were picking a pen pal for the first time?

2) When Juanita received Anne's letter, she said that it was written in English. Why do you think it was written in English?

3) Years went by with no letter back from Anne. If you were Juanita, would you think something bad happened to Anne? Would you think Anne just forgot to write you? How would you respond?

4) In the letter back from Otto, he explains that the Frank family was taken to a concentration camp because they were Jewish. Juanita had finally got her answer to the question of why Anne stopped writing. In which ways does the story have a sad ending? In which ways did Anne's story help educate the world? How has Anne Frank inspired or motivated the world? Do you think she ever imagined that the whole world would read her diary as she wrote it?

Extended Activities

A) The author uses a lot of expression and feeling words in this story, such as anxiety, puzzlement, curiosity, excitement and relief. Type these (and other) emotion words on different pieces of paper. Give one to each student (or group of students) and let them act out their word. The other students or groups can try to guess the emotion that is acted out. For further comprehension, have the students give examples of situations of when they would feel the emotion.

B) In one of her letters to Juanita, Anne mentioned her hobby of postcard collecting. At the Danville Station museum in Iowa (Juanita's hometown), they are collecting postcards sent from around the world in honor of Anne Frank and others who lost their lives in the Holocaust. Have your students write a postcard from your hometown with the lesson they learned from the story on the back.

Danville Schools
c/o Janet Hesler
419 S Main Street
Danville, Iowa 52623

C) On the website **www.traces.org/anne.html**, there are copies of the letters that Anne sent Juanita. Read one of the letters aloud. Have the student pretend they are Juanita and write a response to Anne's letter. Make sure to review the rules of letter writing. Every letter should include a heading, greeting, body, closing, and signature.

LEARNING STATION

Bullying Definition

According to Olweus Bullying Prevention Program: "A person is bullied when he or she is exposed, repeatedly and over time, to negative actions on the part of one or more other persons, and he or she has difficulty defending himself or herself."

Discussion Questions Relating to Bullying

Do you see an example of bullying in *Oceans Apart*?
How does this story compare to bullying situations in your own school and community?
What can you do to stop bullying from taking place?

Anti-Bullying Role Playing

Role playing is a way for students to internalize different responses and practices to reduce conflict in social situations. Review the possible coping strategies with students. Discuss how to deal with a specific bullying situation. Once the group decides on an appropriate coping strategy(s), students can act it out. Take note that the bully could react in a variety of different ways.

4 words to describe emotion:
- cheated
- frightened
- pressured
- unfairly treated

Situation: A girl is standing on the playground at recess playing catch with a friend. A girl who is bullying approaches to demand the use of the ball. How should the first girl respond?

Bullying Coping Strategies

- **Avoidance** – Find a way to ignore the bully. Sometimes attention is what the bully wants.
- **Assertiveness** – Sometimes the best way to deal with a bully is to defend yourself by telling them to leave you alone. If you are watching someone else being bullied, stand up for that person.
- **Friendship** – Strength in numbers will sometimes put a bully in his/her place. Find someone who will stand up with you. Be the person who defends a victim of a bully.
- **Education** – Find an adult (teacher, parent, mentor, etc.) to help you educate others about treating all people with respect. If a bully won't back down, get someone with authority to help you stop the situation.

Advice from the Wagner's Story

Take time to reach out to someone different from you. Write a note to that person today. Have students discuss and/or write how this advice could be used in their life.

LEARNING STATION

Comprehension Questions

Cite evidence from the story text in your answers.

1. Have you ever had a pen pal? _____
_____
_____
_____

2. Why did Juanita have butterflies when she drew her pen pal's name? _____
_____
_____
_____

3. What did Anne say in her letter to Juanita? _____
_____
_____
_____

4. What did Betty Ann say to Juanita during the phone call? _____
_____
_____
_____

5. What does Jewish mean? _____
_____

6. What happened to Anne and her family? _____
_____
_____
_____

7. Why will Juanita always remember her experience with Anne? _____
_____

8. What did you learn from Juanita's story? _____
_____
_____
_____

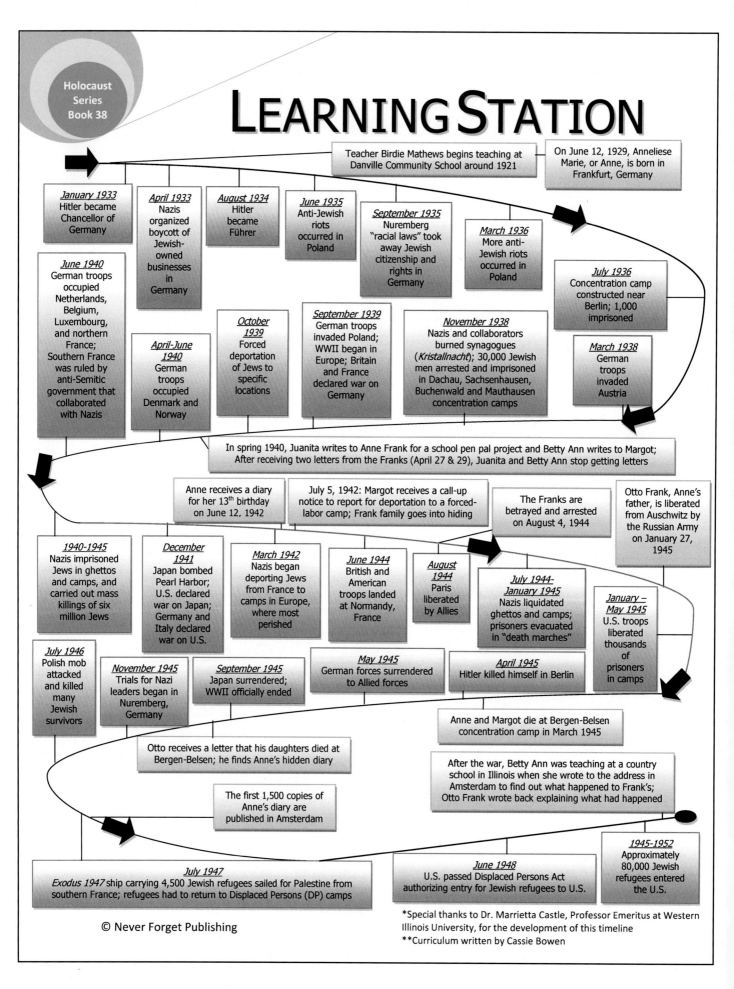

LEARNING STATION

Holocaust Series Book 38

Teacher Birdie Mathews begins teaching at Danville Community School around 1921

On June 12, 1929, Anneliese Marie, or Anne, is born in Frankfurt, Germany

January 1933
Hitler became Chancellor of Germany

April 1933
Nazis organized boycott of Jewish-owned businesses in Germany

August 1934
Hitler became Führer

June 1935
Anti-Jewish riots occurred in Poland

September 1935
Nuremberg "racial laws" took away Jewish citizenship and rights in Germany

March 1936
More anti-Jewish riots occurred in Poland

July 1936
Concentration camp constructed near Berlin; 1,000 imprisoned

June 1940
German troops occupied Netherlands, Belgium, Luxembourg, and northern France; Southern France was ruled by anti-Semitic government that collaborated with Nazis

April-June 1940
German troops occupied Denmark and Norway

October 1939
Forced deportation of Jews to specific locations

September 1939
German troops invaded Poland; WWII began in Europe; Britain and France declared war on Germany

November 1938
Nazis and collaborators burned synagogues (*Kristallnacht*); 30,000 Jewish men arrested and imprisoned in Dachau, Sachsenhausen, Buchenwald and Mauthausen concentration camps

March 1938
German troops invaded Austria

In spring 1940, Juanita writes to Anne Frank for a school pen pal project and Betty Ann writes to Margot; After receiving two letters from the Franks (April 27 & 29), Juanita and Betty Ann stop getting letters

Anne receives a diary for her 13th birthday on June 12, 1942

July 5, 1942: Margot receives a call-up notice to report for deportation to a forced-labor camp; Frank family goes into hiding

The Franks are betrayed and arrested on August 4, 1944

Otto Frank, Anne's father, is liberated from Auschwitz by the Russian Army on January 27, 1945

1940-1945
Nazis imprisoned Jews in ghettos and camps, and carried out mass killings of six million Jews

December 1941
Japan bombed Pearl Harbor; U.S. declared war on Japan; Germany and Italy declared war on U.S.

March 1942
Nazis began deporting Jews from France to camps in Europe, where most perished

June 1944
British and American troops landed at Normandy, France

August 1944
Paris liberated by Allies

July 1944-January 1945
Nazis liquidated ghettos and camps; prisoners evacuated in "death marches"

January – May 1945
U.S. troops liberated thousands of prisoners in camps

July 1946
Polish mob attacked and killed many Jewish survivors

November 1945
Trials for Nazi leaders began in Nuremberg, Germany

September 1945
Japan surrendered; WWII officially ended

May 1945
German forces surrendered to Allied forces

April 1945
Hitler killed himself in Berlin

Anne and Margot die at Bergen-Belsen concentration camp in March 1945

Otto receives a letter that his daughters died at Bergen-Belsen; he finds Anne's hidden diary

After the war, Betty Ann was teaching at a country school in Illinois when she wrote to the address in Amsterdam to find out what happened to Frank's; Otto Frank wrote back explaining what had happened

The first 1,500 copies of Anne's diary are published in Amsterdam

July 1947
Exodus 1947 ship carrying 4,500 Jewish refugees sailed for Palestine from southern France; refugees had to return to Displaced Persons (DP) camps

June 1948
U.S. passed Displaced Persons Act authorizing entry for Jewish refugees to U.S.

1945-1952
Approximately 80,000 Jewish refugees entered the U.S.

© Never Forget Publishing

*Special thanks to Dr. Marrietta Castle, Professor Emeritus at Western Illinois University, for the development of this timeline
**Curriculum written by Cassie Bowen

A BOOK by ME®
OPERATION WRITE NOW

"I'm asking ordinary children to do something extraordinary!"

Deb Bowen, Creator & Director
www.abookbyme.com

I'm asking ordinary children all over the world to use their talents to share extraordinary stories. Many students write about Holocaust survivors, Righteous Gentiles (non-Jews who risked their lives to save the Jewish people), prison camp liberators and other important stories of World War II. Since this generation is getting older, the time to interview them, write and illustrate their important story is RIGHT NOW!

Some students are deciding to tell important stories about human rights or heroes as well. Check out the website and then decide what interests you. The writer's guidelines are online, and you can register your story once you decide who your subject will be. Also, online you will find a sample of a newspaper article you could use to find a subject in your hometown. Talking to a grandparent, visiting nursing homes, VFW or meeting with a local historian might lead you to a possible story.

All authors / illustrators must be age 18 or under to qualify. All submissions will be given consideration for the A BOOK by ME series, but there is no guarantee the work will be published.

It is my hope you have learned from the book you just read and are interested in reading more work by young authors. It would delight me to know you are inspired to write a book about a subject important to you.

Be careful and watch yourselves closely so you do not forget the things your eyes have seen or let them slip from your heart as long as you live. Teach them to your children and to your children's children.
Deuteronomy 4:9

CYA Calling Youth to Action

1 Kouski's Kids

The War and the Boy shares the remarkable experiences of Roy Kouski, an American soldier in Europe during World War II. Roy's moving story was written by his granddaughter, Brittany Ern. CYA challenges young people who love writing or art to take part in a book project through A BOOK by ME. Make Roy and Brittany proud by becoming one of Kouski's Kids! Check out the writer's guidelines at www.abookbyme.com.

2 Mwalimu's Dream

Mwalimu, a young man from Kenya, came to the USA as a foreign exchange student and went home a young author through A BOOK by ME. Read Mwalimu's Dream to learn how he changed thousands of lives in his village with the gift of clean water. There are still many villages that need wells. CYA hopes your classroom is moved to contribute spare change to dig water wells in undeveloped countries. Your small change can make a big change in someone's life! Take a look at www.wells4wellness.com.

3 Change the World

After World War II, student exchange was created to encourage foreign youth to study in the United States. Exchange provides opportunities to build relationships and share cultures which creates better understanding and mutual respect. People whose countries have been former enemies have become "family" through exchange. Hosts are responsible to provide room and board, love and support. The student provides his/her own spending money and health insurance. Host families are always needed. Contact dbowenexchange@gmail.com to learn more.